Play-Along Trumpet

World Music

Cuba

Richard Graf & Richard Filz

Piano reduction by Martin Reiter

Audio Download

Auf der Website www.universaledition.com/ue38733-service steht das Audio-Material (Vollversion und Play-along) kostenlos zur Verfügung.

The audio material (full version and play-along) can be accessed free of charge at:
www.universaledition.com/ue38733-service

Les pistes audio (version complète et accompagnement) est à votre disposition gratuitement sur notre site :
www.universaledition.com/ue38733-service

Coverfoto: © Look GmbH, München

Musicians:
Walter Fend (Trumpet), Andreas Pirringer (Flute), Richard Graf (Guitar, Bass, Piano),
Richard Filz (Percussion Instruments)

Digital Recording and Mix: RICH ART Productions
Digital Mastering: Richard Graf

Special thanks to Martin Hlatky for technical support.

UE 38733
ISMN 979-0-008-09191-9
UPC 8-03452-07566-0
ISBN 978-3-7024-0072-9

© Copyright 2000, 2008 by Universal Edition AG, Wien

Vorwort

Höre die zum kostenlosen Download bereitstehenden Audiodaten gut an, um die richtige Phrasierung kennen zu lernen. Bei den Play-Along-Versionen kannst du gemeinsam mit dem Originalensemble spielen. Als alternative Begleitung ist eine Klavierstimme abgedruckt, die sowohl von klassisch als auch im Jazz ausgebildeten MusikerInnen gespielt werden kann. Diese Klavierfassung kann von der Ensembleversion geringfügig abweichen. Für andere Begleitinstrumente (z. B. Gitarre) sind Akkordsymbole eingezeichnet.

Preface

Listen carefully to the audio tracks provided to familiarise yourself with the correct phrasing. The play-along versions allow you to play together with the original ensemble. As an alternative accompaniment, the printed music includes a piano part which can be played by both classical and jazz-trained musicians. The piano accompaniment can differ slightly from the ensemble version. For other accompaniment instruments (e.g. guitar), chord symbols are shown.

Préface

Ecoute attentivement les pistes audio ci-joint pour te familiariser avec le phrasé exact. Les versions « Play along » te permettent de jouer avec l'ensemble original. La partie piano est imprimée sous forme d'accompagnement alternatif, elle peut être aussi bien interprétée par les musiciens de formation classique que par les musiciens de jazz. Cette partie piano peut diverger minime de la version ensemble. Des symboles d'accord pour d'autres instruments d'accompagnement (guitare p.ex.) sont indiqués.

Inhalt • Contents • Table des Matières

Bolero	2
Son Montuno	4
Cha Cha	7
Mambo	10
Rumba	14

Bolero

Music: Richard Graf/Richard Filz

Son Montuno

Music: Richard Graf/Richard Filz

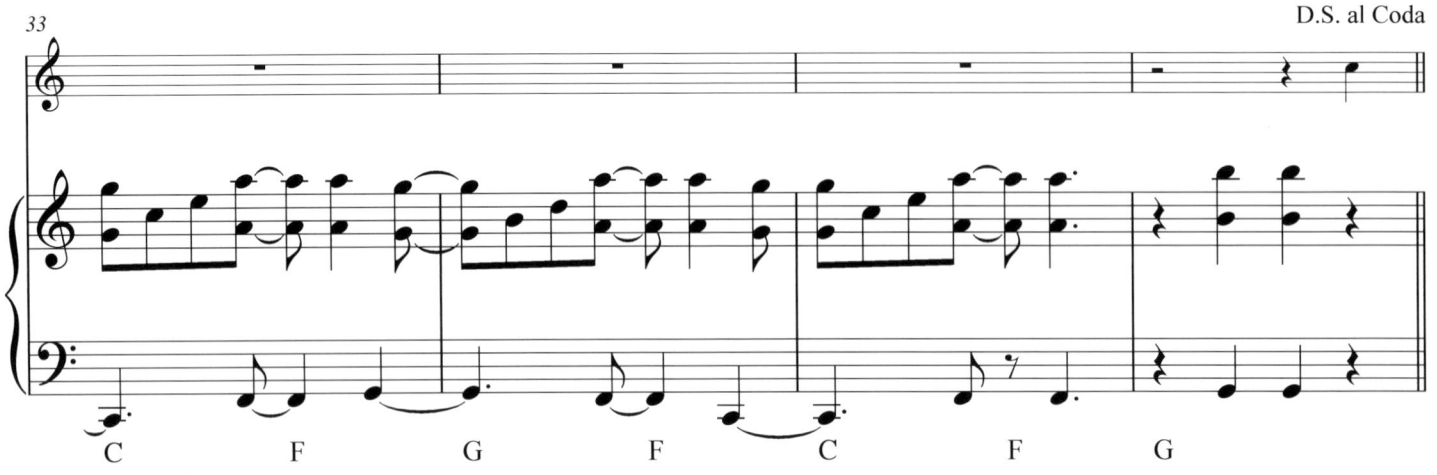

Cha Cha

Music: Richard Graf/Richard Filz

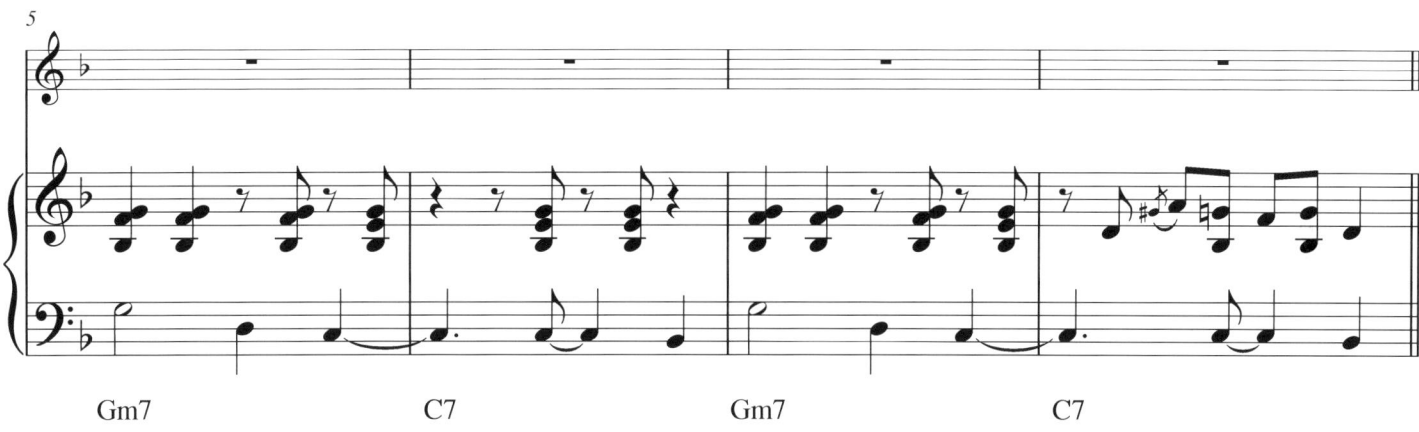

© Copyright 2000, 2008 by Universal Edition AG, Wien

UE 38 733

Trumpet

Bolero

CD Track 1/2
Music: Richard Graf/Richard Filz

Son Montuno

CD Track 3/4
Music: Richard Graf/Richard Filz

© Copyright 2000, 2008 by Universal Edition AG, Wien

Universal Edition UE 38 733 a

Cha Cha

CD Track 5/6
Music: Richard Graf/Richard Filz

Mambo

CD Track 7/8
Music: Richard Graf/Richard Filz

Rumba

CD Track 9/10
Music: Richard Graf/Richard Filz

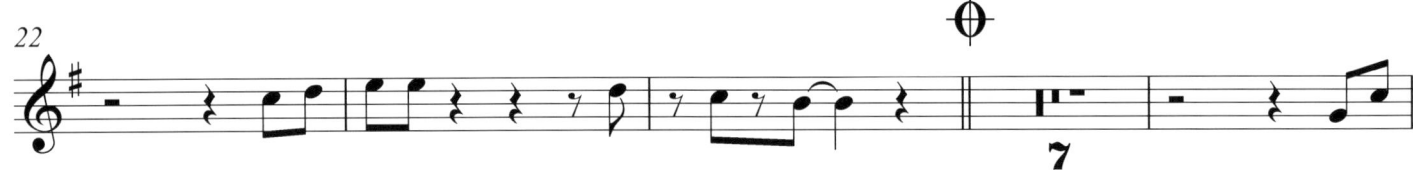
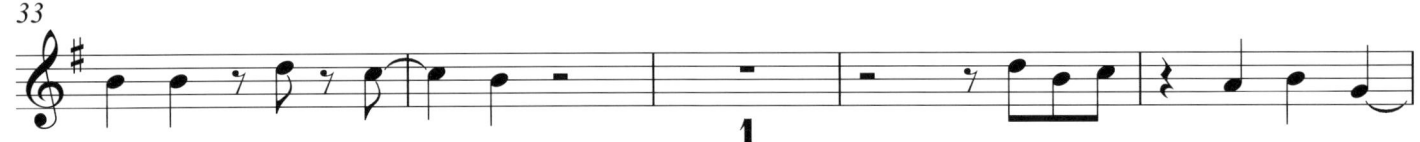

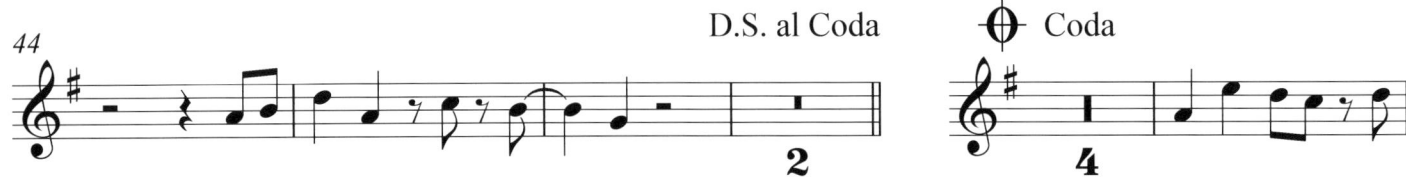

© Copyright 2000, 2008 by Universal Edition AG, Wien

Universal Edition UE 38 733 a

Mambo

Music: Richard Graf/Richard Filz

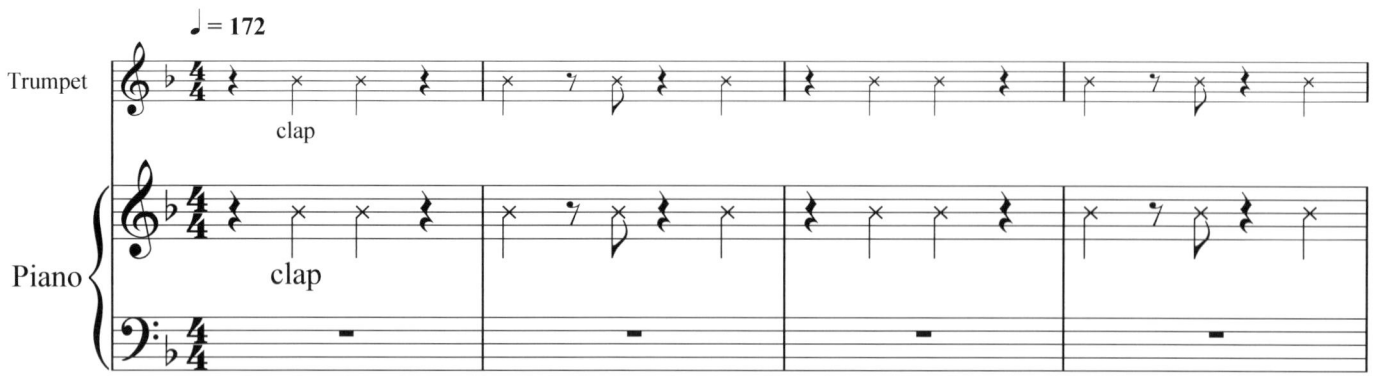

Rumba

Music: Richard Graf/Richard Filz

World Music – Ensemble

Instrumentation:

Melody I in C & B♭
Melody II in C & B♭
Piano
Guitar
Bass
Percussion ad lib.

Cuba
Richard Graf & Richard Filz
Bolero, Mambo, Cha Cha, Son Montuno, Rumba
Schwierigkeitsgrad 2
UE 31521

Ireland
Richard Graf
The Wild Rover, The Foggy Dew, Danny Boy, The Wind That Shakes the Barley, The Connaughtman's Rambles
Schwierigkeitsgrad 2
UE 31522

Israel
Timna Brauer & Elias Meiri
Tchiribim Tchiribom, Shalosh bnot hapele, Dror Yikra, Ahavat Hadassa, Hava Nagila
Schwierigkeitsgrad 2
UE 31523

Russia
Iwan Malachowskij
Kalinka, Schwarze Augen, Der Mond scheint, Steppe rund herum, Valenky
Schwierigkeitsgrad 2
UE 31524

Scotland
James Rae
Scotland the Brave, My Love is like a Red, Red Rose, The Skye Boat Song, Mhairi's Wedding, 100 Pipers
Schwierigkeitsgrad 2
UE 31525

Brazil
Jovino Santos Neto
Choro da Luz, Maracatu, Cantigas de Roda, Quebrasamba, Coco
Schwierigkeitsgrad 3
UE 31526

Madagascar
HAJAmadagascar & August Schmidhofer
Apondo, E! Ralinina, O! Dralako, Zahoravo, Fiainana
Schwierigkeitsgrad 3
UE 31527

Argentina
Diego Collatti
Tango, Vals Criollo, Milonga, Chacarera, Zamba
Schwierigkeitsgrad 3
UE 31528

Klezmer
Yale Strom
The Silver Crown, Ma Yofes, Romanian Hora, Stoliner Nign, Dorohoi Khusidl
Schwierigkeitsgrad 3
UE 31529

vienna • london • new york

649 / XII 07